HOW TO DRAW FANTASY ART

WARRIORS

Steve Beaumont

FRANKLIN WATTS
LONDON • SYDNEY

First published in 2007 by Franklin Watts

Copyright © 2007 Arcturus Publishing Limited

Franklin Watts
338 Euston Road
London NW1 3BH

Franklin Watts Australia
Level 17/207 Kent St, Sydney, NSW 2000

Produced by Arcturus Publishing Limited,
26/27 Bickels Yard, 151–153 Bermondsey Street, London SE1 3HA

Artwork and text: Steve Beaumont
Editor: Alex Woolf
Designer: Jane Hawkins

A CIP catalogue record for this book is available from the British Library.

Dewey Decimal Classification Number: 743'.87

ISBN: 978 0 7496 7654 4

Printed in China

Franklin Watts is a division of Hachette Children's Books.

Contents

Introduction

If you've picked up this book, you are probably a big fan of sword-and-sorcery movies, books or games. You may be one of those fans who enjoys the genre so much that you'd like to have a go at creating some magical characters for yourself. If so, this book will help you get started on the right path.

One of the best things about drawing warriors and other fantasy figures is that – apart from the basic rules of anatomy and perspective – there are no other rules. In fantasy art, no one can tell you that a character's sword is the wrong shape or his hair is the wrong colour – these are products of your imagination and you can draw them exactly as you please!

Warriors

Warriors play a central role in many myths and legends. They are usually brave and heroic characters who go on dangerous quests to right wrongs, fight dragons and rescue damsels. The most interesting warriors often possess some flaw in their character. Sir Lancelot's weakness was for the wife of his king. Samson was undone by his own pride.

In this book we will encounter some warriors who might appear more anti-hero than hero, but who ultimately fight for the greater good, perhaps sacrificing themselves in the process.

Equipment

To start with, you'll need the tools of the trade. Decent materials and equipment are essential if you want to produce high-quality illustrations.

Paper

For your practice sketches, buy some cheap A4 or A3 paper from a stationery shop. When practising ink drawing, use line art paper, which can be purchased from an art or craft shop.

For painting with watercolours, use watercolour paper. Most art shops stock a large range of weights and sizes – 250 g/m or 300 g/m is fine.

Pencils

Get a good range of lead pencils ranging from soft (6B) to hard (2H). Hard-leaded pencils last longer and leave fewer smudges on your paper. Soft-leaded ones leave darker marks on the paper and wear down more quickly. 2H pencils are a good medium-range product to start with.

For fine, detailed work, mechanical pencils are ideal. These are available in a range of lead thicknesses, 0.5 mm being a good middle range.

Pens

For inking, use either a ballpoint or a simple dip pen and nib. For colouring, experiment with the wide variety of felt-tips on the market.

Markers

These are very versatile pens that, with practice, can give very pleasing results.

Brushes

Some artists like to use a fine brush for inking line work. This takes a bit more practice to master, but the results can be very satisfying. If you want to try your hand at brushwork, you will need some good-quality sable brushes.

Watercolours and gouache

Most art shops will also stock a wide range of these products from student to professional quality.

Inks

Any good brand will do.

Eraser

There are three types of eraser: rubber, plastic and putty. Try all three to see which you prefer.

INDIAN INK

Oh, and you may need something for sharpening your pencils…

Basic Construction

Here's a pencil drawing of a valiant warrior striking a heroic pose. Great! But how do we get from a blank piece of paper to this? The answer lies in mastering the basic stick figure. If you can draw the stick figure effectively, everything else flows from there. This skill is particularly important when drawing action scenes, where your figurework needs to be full of energy.

The sketches below show the stages of the process that resulted in the drawing on the previous page.

Step 1

First, produce some loose sketches (called thumbnails) to establish the basic shape of the figure. Then make a larger drawing of your chosen sketch.

Step 2

The basic construction of the human form can be broken down into geometric shapes, such as squares, circles and triangles. When drawing these shapes it helps to think of them as solid objects – spheres, egg shapes, cubes and cylinders. Now try using these shapes to flesh out your stick figure.

Step 3

Finally, add a smoother finish to the stick figure.

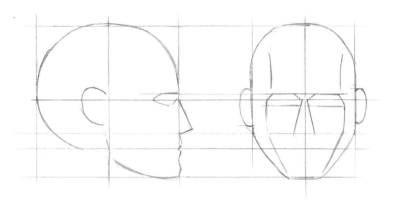

Faces, Hands and Feet

As with all character drawing, so much of the personality of a warrior is to be found in the face. It's therefore worth spending a bit of time honing your techniques in this crucial area. Hands and feet are also very important in action illustrations, and can be quite tricky to get right.

Constructing the face

The human head generally fits into a square. Note that the nose and chin protrude slightly. It may help to divide the square into quarters. The eyes generally sit halfway above the centre line, with the nose taking up half the depth of the bottom square. Note the alignment of the ears in relation to the eyes and nose.

Male face

Our hero is looking down and a little to the side, so draw an upside-down egg shape for his head, and place it at a slight angle. Draw in lines to help you position the eyes, nose and mouth. It helps to think of it as a 3-D egg while you do this.

Female face

As much as we like our
male warriors handsome, we
like our female warriors to be beautiful. Try to
make the face a little thinner and more refined
than the male warrior. The mouth should be smaller and
the lips fuller.

Hands

A good way of becoming better acquainted with this part of the anatomy is to
practise drawing your own hand in different positions. Essentially, the palm is
square-ish. Split the fingers into three sections. The same goes for the thumb, but
draw its base section as a large triangle. This is not anatomically accurate, but it does
help when sketching hand movements.

Feet

This is a part of the body
that a lot of budding artists
struggle with. In most cases,
just think of the foot as a
sort of triangular shape.
Use these examples as a
guide to its construction.

Male Warrior

Although a heroic figure, this particular warrior is also bordering on the barbaric. He is a true fighter who lives for the thrill of battle. Muscular and brutish, he will stop at nothing to defeat his enemies.

Stage 1
Start with your stick figure. Lower the head and widen the stance to make an aggressive pose.

Stage 2
Bulk out your stick figure with geometric shapes to create the basis of a muscular-looking warrior.

Stage 3
Work on the face. Make him look fierce but not ugly. A rugged handsomeness is what you're after, with a square jaw and unruly hair.

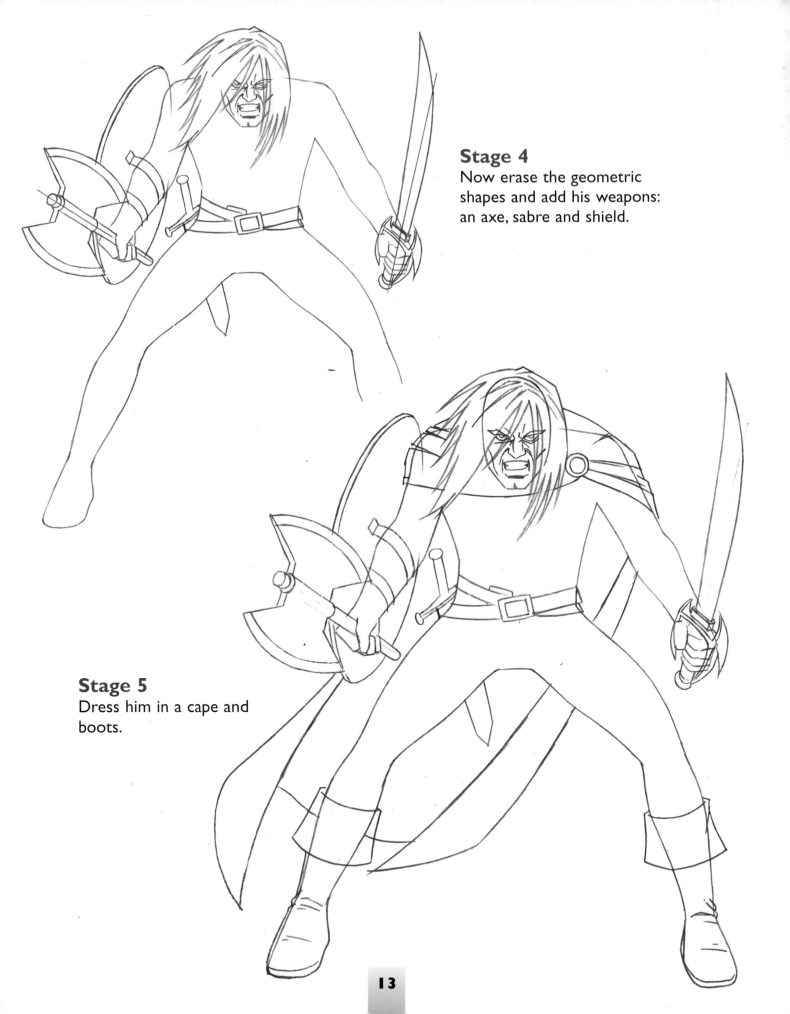

Stage 4
Now erase the geometric shapes and add his weapons: an axe, sabre and shield.

Stage 5
Dress him in a cape and boots.

Stage 6

Add a leather breastplate with an emblem or insignia on it. Design your own, if you wish.

Stage 7

Refine the earlier pencil work and add in some shading to give your figure solidity.

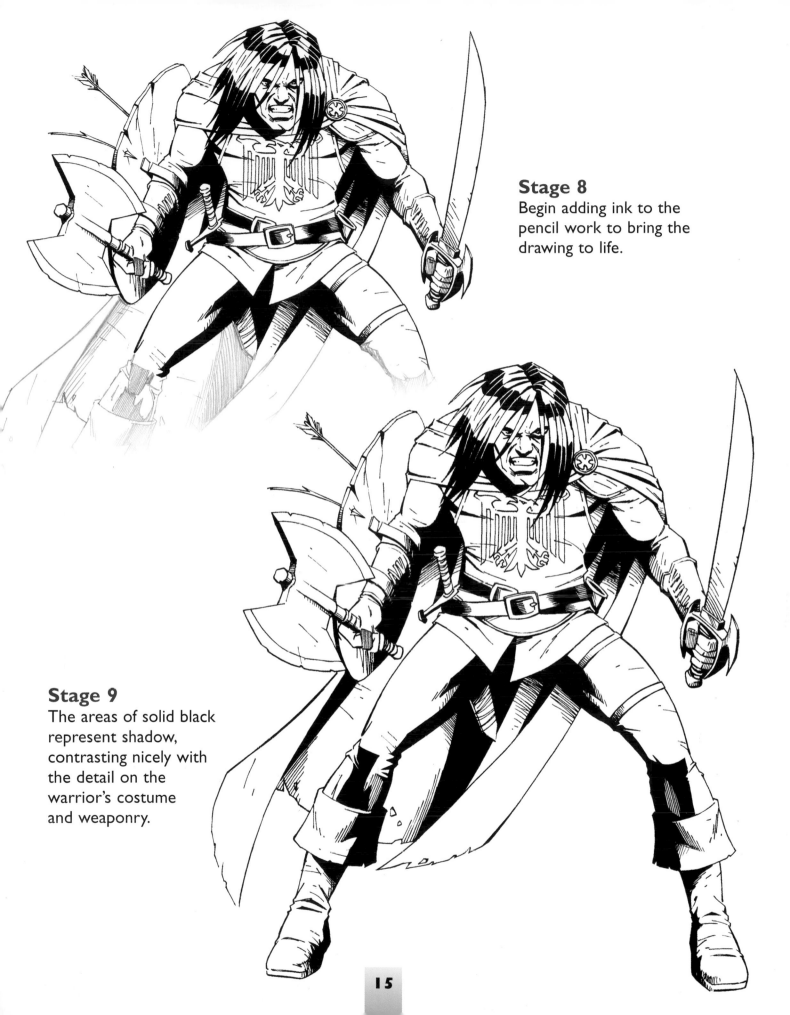

Stage 8
Begin adding ink to the pencil work to bring the drawing to life.

Stage 9
The areas of solid black represent shadow, contrasting nicely with the detail on the warrior's costume and weaponry.

Stage 10

You can colour your drawing, if you like, using marker pens, felt-tips or watercolours. Lay down each colour in one continuous wash if you can, applying the colour as smoothly as possible.

Keeping to dull, darker colours will add to the overall impression of a savage warrior about to attack. You wouldn't want to be on the other end of that sword, would you?

Female Warrior

Who says only guys should have all the orc-slaying fun? Girls can swing an axe with the best of them. History is littered with female warriors, from Boudicca, Queen of the Britons, to Joan of Arc, the fearless leader of the French — and that's fact, not fantasy!

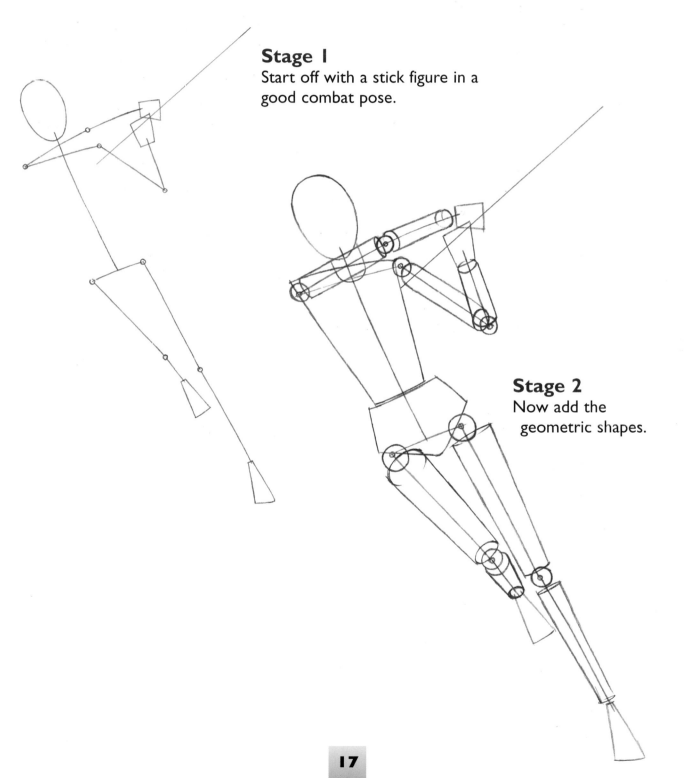

Stage 1
Start off with a stick figure in a good combat pose.

Stage 2
Now add the geometric shapes.

Stage 3

Give her shape and definition by adding the outer form. Work on the face and hair. Note how the curve of her eyebrows and the frown lines on her forehead give her a fierce and determined expression.

Stage 4

Now let's give her a chain mail tunic for protection, and some boots. And don't forget the axe!

Stage 5

Here is the finished pencil drawing. Note the added detail on her chain mail, weaponry, boots and hair.

Stage 6

Now clean up the line work and carefully ink over the pencil drawing, making sure you keep the lines crisp and clean.

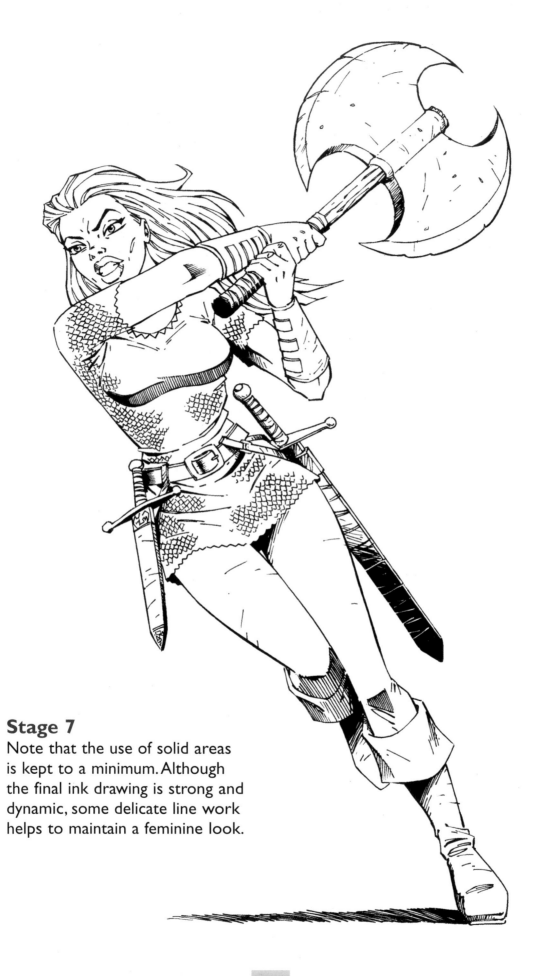

Stage 7
Note that the use of solid areas is kept to a minimum. Although the final ink drawing is strong and dynamic, some delicate line work helps to maintain a feminine look.

Stage 8

Now you can colour your drawing.
The flame-red hair emphasizes our heroine's
warrior nature. Traditionally, female warriors are
illustrated using lighter colours, with fewer dark
or dull tones.

Warrior on Horseback

This hero appears more savage than noble — a nomadic warrior on horseback, roaming from kingdom to kingdom in search of adventure.

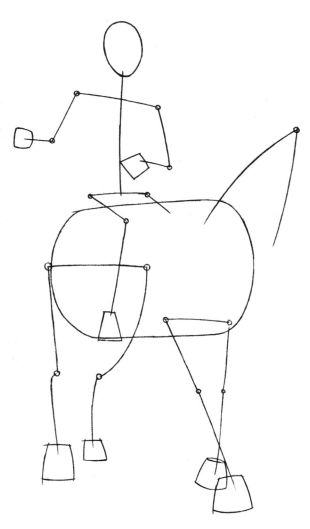

Stage 1

This image may look complex, but it's far less daunting when broken down into easy stages. Because the skeleton of a horse is not as straightforward as the human skeleton – and not totally essential to producing this image – the horse will be broken down into a frame that's not technically correct, but will make drawing it much easier. Start with your stick figure.

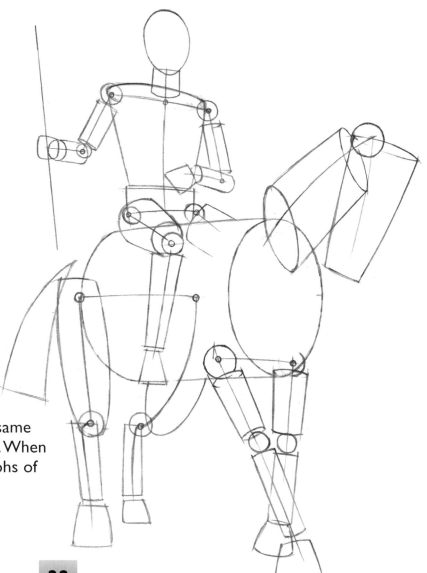

Stage 2

Note how a horse can be formed from the same geometric shapes as a human figure. A long, bulky cylinder is used for the horse's body, while the legs follow the same ball-joint construction as for human figures. When drawing animals it helps to study photographs of the creature that you wish to draw and try breaking it down into geometric shapes.

Stage 3

Produce a smoother outer form over the geometric shapes. Narrow eyes and a square jaw create the right mood for this warrior.

Stage 4

Now erase the geometric shapes and add a full head of unruly black hair, plus a fur around his shoulders and a leather vest. Also add the horse's mane.

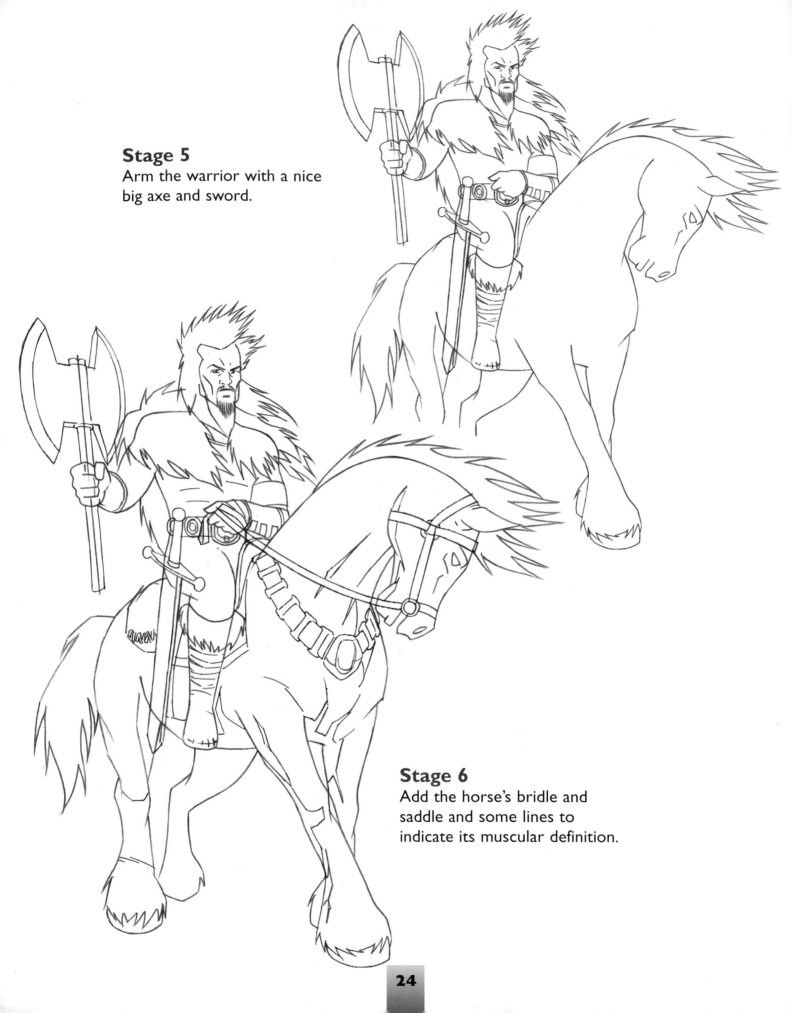

Stage 5
Arm the warrior with a nice big axe and sword.

Stage 6
Add the horse's bridle and saddle and some lines to indicate its muscular definition.

Stage 7

Put in the final details to your pencil drawing. Shade the darker areas and clean up any rough line work.

Stage 8

Now start the inking, being careful not to lose any of the smaller details by overdoing it.

Stage 9

Note the use of solid black on areas such as the horse's rear legs to create depth. The deep shadows add to the sense of brooding menace in both warrior and steed.

Stage 10
Although it may be tempting to use only dark colours with this warrior, try breaking up the darker tones with pale browns and yellows, so that the image doesn't look too flat. A light blue wash has been added to the axe, making it appear stronger and heavier.

Warrior Gallery

Here are some examples of warriors of all types, doing what they do best — preparing for battle. Why not try reproducing some of them yourself by breaking them down into stages, as we have done on the previous pages. Alternatively, use them as inspiration for creating your own characters.

Glossary

alignment The positioning of different parts of an object or objects relative to each other.

anatomy The physical structure of a human or other organism.

ball joint Also known as a ball-and-socket joint, this is a joint in which the rounded end of one parts fits into a cup-shaped socket on the other.

barbaric Uncivilized and primitive.

Boudicca A queen of the Britons and ruler of the Iceni tribe, who led her forces in a revolt against the Romans in 60–61 CE.

bridle A set of leather straps fitted to a horse's head, including the bit and the reins.

brutish Like an animal.

chain mail Interlinked rings of metal forming a flexible piece of armour.

cylinder A shape with straight sides and circular ends of equal size.

dynamic Full of energy.

emblem A visual symbol, such as a badge, that represents a person, group or organization.

geometric shape Simple shapes, such as cubes, spheres and cylinders.

gouache A mixture of non-transparent watercolour paint and gum.

insignia An identifying mark or badge.

Joan of Arc A French national heroine who led the French armies against the English during the Hundred Years War, relieving the besieged city of Orléans in 1429.

mechanical pencil A pencil with replaceable lead that may be advanced as needed.

nomadic Describing a person who wanders from one place to another.

orc A member of an imaginary race of ugly, warlike and evil creatures.

perspective In drawing, changing the relative size and appearance of objects to allow for the effects of distance.

protrude Stick out.

sabre A heavy sword with a slightly curved blade that is sharp on one edge.

sacrifice A giving up of something valuable or important – even your life – for the sake of someone or something else.

Samson An Israelite warrior from Biblical times, famous for his great strength.

Sir Lancelot A legendary warrior, the most famous of King Arthur's knights.

sphere An object shaped like a ball.

stance The way a person stands.

steed A horse, especially a lively, spirited one.

stick figure A simple drawing of a person with single lines for the torso, arms and legs.

tone Any of the possible shades of a particular colour.

torso The upper part of the human body, not including the head and arms.

valiant Brave and steadfast.

watercolour Paint made by mixing pigments (substances that give something its colour) with water.

Further Information

Books

Drawing and Painting Fantasy Figures: From the Imagination to the Page by Finlay Cowan (David and Charles, 2004)

Draw Medieval Fantasies by Damon J. Reinagle (Peel Productions, 1995)

How to Draw Comic Book Bad Guys and Gals by Christopher Hart (Watson-Guptill Publications, 1998)

How to Draw Comic Book Heroes and Villains by Christopher Hart (Watson-Guptill Publications, 2001)

How to Draw Fantasy Characters by Christopher Hart (Watson-Guptill Publications, 1999)

How to Draw Manga Heroes and Villains by Peter Gray (Watts, 2005)

Websites

drawsketch.about.com/od/drawfantasyandscifi/tp/imagination.htm
Advice on drawing from the imagination.

elfwood.lysator.liu.se/farp/art.html
An online guide to creating your own fantasy art.

Note to parents and teachers:

Every effort has been made by the publishers to ensure that these websites are suitable for children and contain no inappropriate or offensive material. However, because of the nature of the Internet, it is impossible to guarantee that the contents of these sites will not be altered. We strongly advise that Internet access is supervised by a responsible adult.

Index